Interrogations

Leroy V. Quintana

ISBN: 0-9628524-5-7

Twelve of these poems appeared, in a different format, in *Five Poets of Aztlan*, Santiago Daydí-Tolson, ed. (Arizona State University, Bilingual Review/Press: Tempe, AZ) 198. Three others appeared in *Men of Our Time: An Anthology of Male Poetry in Contemporary America* (University of Georgia Press, 1992).

Viet Nam Generation, Inc.
&
Burning Cities Press
2921 Terrace Drive
Chevy Chase, MD   20815

in cooperation with Pratt Publishing Company, Inc.

This book was produced on a Macintosh IIcx computer with 8 mgs of RAM, a 105mg Quantum internal hard drive, a Syquest 44mg removable media cartridge drive, and a Radius 19" grey-scale monitor. Camera-ready copy was printed by an Apple LaserWriter IINTX on Strathmore Legacy paper. Software used in production ran under System 6.07 and included Microsoft Word 4.0, PageMaker 4.0 and Adobe PhotoShop 1.07. Typefonts are Impressum and Garamond. Offset printing and binding was done by BookMasters, Inc. of Mansfield, OH.

This book is dedicated to the men and women
who served in Viet Nam.

And to my wife, Yolanda, and David A. Willson,
whose support made this book possible.

Contents

The Nam

Ten Years After

Ten Years After

Introduction

In a time of long, overly researched discursive narratives constructed on borrowed pathos, Leroy Quintana has given us this tapestry of small moments that explode and fragment. His poetry seems to have been written through old eyes, a mature heart, with a perspective untouched by the contemporary flare for ego and surface intellect. A youthful telling sparked by a *need*, however, is what gives these earned words and revelations their energy and weight. These are poems where the various characters walk out of the white space to assume a real life. There's flesh on each metaphor. Through direct language and simplicity, Quintana gives us poems that attempt to defy the school of pumped up abstractions and intellectual masturbation. Here we are confronted by those who were condemned as witnesses and participants in the tragedy of the Viet Nam war (what the Viets refer to as The American War).

Interrogations isn't a treatise on clever obscurity and evasion; thus we should thank this poet for his commitment to facing some painful truths—without any flippancy to distract and short circuit the telling. Here's a genius for clarity that avoids convenient resolutions.

There isn't any flab on these poems. Consider the raw language that bloodflowers in "Daley":

> Daley had to hump the boonies with the clap;
> his dick hanging out,
> wrapped in a plastic bag to catch the drip.
> A sorrowful Christ carrying a cross
> tattooed on his biceps.

Quoted in its entirety, this poem reverberates with realism. We can see Daley; we know him.

Many of Quintana's poems are titled with names, giving us lively characters that refuse dehumanization through false gestures. I believe and trust these poems composed from the lives of common folk of diverse origins: "Atkins was a cowboy from Oklahoma," "Kirby knew tobacco," "Benny came back unbelieving," and so on. This tessellation of names and images accretes into a world that is worth the attention of anyone who is interested in the Viet Nam war and good poetry. Leroy Quintana's poems, these shards of penetrating clarity, are filled with surprises that force us to question ourselves.

—Yusef Komunyakaa

Preface

Benito

Benito, so thin he looked almost starved,
had been a prisoner of war in Korea.
His dark eyes hard, forgiving, kindly, indifferent.
Softspoken if he said anything at all.
It was rumored he had been tortured.
We students of the Catholic school were forever selling
Christmas seals, magazine subscriptions, etc.
The nuns told us God had spared Benito's life,
and that he should be eternally grateful.
But he always politely turned us down.
Sister Rita thought he was an infidel.
He never bought as much as a raffle ticket.

Sammy

Sammy, who had been in combat in World War II,
wore a false leg; half of him was bowlegged.
Everyday, all day long he worked on cars,
and sped back and forth gruffly in his battered pickup
for parts, as well as for cheap whiskey, Coors.
Day after day.
A hero, especially to us, the young boys
who stopped their play only for him.
His fretful, contentious eyes
shattered as his windshield.

How It Was Going To Be

Armed Forces Recruitment Day
Albuquerque High School, 1962

After the Navy,
the Air Force, and
the Army,
Sgt. Castillo,
the Marine Corps
recruiter,
got a standing ovation
when he walked up
to the microphone
and said proudly
that unlike
the rest, all
he could promise
was a pack,
a rifle, and
a damned hard time.
Except for that,
he was the
biggest
of liars.

Nomenclature

Got a new name,
also Government Issue,
to go with all that olive green.
Everyone a swinging dick.
Swinging Richard
when a Drill Sergeant
felt like being erudite.

Drill Sergeant Price

Every morning wave after wave of NVAs,
mines taped to their chests,
came rushing at him.
You could see them
in his bleached, hardened eyes.
To teach us to stay awake,
if the Army would've let him have his way,
he would've pulled a pin from a grenade,
have one in our midst hold it,
see if during the lectures on tactics and weapons
we got so much as a blink of sleep.
We would snicker, wait,
until he stopped muttering,
perhaps praying to himself,
then suddenly call us to attention,
tell us how it was going to be
in Viet Nam.

Pitkin

Out of the hills of Kentucky
or the Sunday Comics, Beetle Bailey.

It was hard to tell.
The difference

between him and Zero
was exactly that.

Drill Sergeant Guerrier

This is what the sergeant said:
Tell them, if they should ask
what you did in Viet Nam,
you were in real estate.

Owned some ground one day,
didn't the next.

Drill Sergeant Brashears

His very name made us afraid; we feared his wrath.
Warned us that whatever God giveth,
he, the top sergeant, could taketh away.
We paid attention when he called us to.
His duty was to teach us the tactics of war.
When it came time for him to send us to Viet Nam,
his eyes rimmed with tears; stern, dutiful eyes
that had never seen combat.

Ralphie

Ralphie was signed up at seventeen
by a fast-talking recruiting sergeant.
Instead of the world got Georgia,
"Airborne" tattooed on his scrawny biceps,
the clap, and caught breaking into footlockers,
another discharge, dishonorable.

Benny

Benny walked around Basic Training bent over.
A right angle almost the entire eight weeks.
Slipped, he said, on the barrack stairs.
Drill Sergeants on his back constantly
couldn't straighten him out.
The same with one doctor, two, several specialists.
We got in from the field one day,
and those on sick call still laughing.
Benny had been given a medical discharge,
called a cab, and walked straight out of the Army,
home.

First Blood

The last week of Basic Training came, final tests.
Drill Sergeant Droke had the platoon chip in,
sent the squad leaders to the PX for sanitary napkins
to protect our elbows during the low crawl.

Afterwards, we peeled the clot-stained tatters off
and were called to attention,
ready now to march off to the fields of valor,
having shed our first blood for the fatherland.

Pitts

First day of AIT,
filled out forms,
and Pitts,
who hailed
from Mississippi
wrote after RACE:
WHITE, and nothing
the Top Sergeant
or anybody else
said could
convince him
he wasn't.

Jump School—First Day

When the Sgt.,
who hadn't
said a word
about them
to anybody else,
saw that Teran
had BORN TO SUFFER
tattooed on his chest,
he made him drop,
give him twenty,
guaranteed him
he'd suffer here,
if for no other
reason.

Jump School—Detail

Saturday morning detail.
The Sgt. handed out
swing rakes.
The grass
tall behind,
between,
the barracks,
waiting.
Mexican lawnmowers,
he called them,
chuckling.

Jump School—
On a Beautiful Day Like This

One Saturday morning
in the Company PX,
a PFC telling
another how,
on a beautiful
day like this
back home,
he and his buddies
would roll tires
over the edge
of the highway
onto the roofs
of Mexicantown.
What fun
to see them
come running out,
so angry,
curses flying

back and forth,
throw them a
finger,
then speed off,
whooping.

Lesson

He had been a bomber pilot in his war
the year I was born
and now he was accompanying me to mine
as far as Seattle.
From there, his vacation in Alaska to hunt bear.
He had known fear
and the fear of being afraid that first time
under fire.
One thing, he kindly told me, you will come to know
when that time comes.
You think you will be the only one,
but always,
there will be someone who is so much more afraid.

Heroic Bronze, Silver Stars

Mother, if it wasn't for our letters
we would never have told
each other much of anything.

We always spoke through objects.
The Boys Book of Famous Soldiers
you gave me one Christmas,
and that small statue of MacArthur.

So I could not tell you.
Instead I called from Fort Lewis,
though I had known since jump school.

And though I would have rather
remained at home, dishonorably,
far better Viet Nam
than you crocheting heroic Bronze, Silver stars
incessantly.

Inspiration

He stormed out of the factory, silver wings
with three stars (each a combat jump
into anti-aircraft fire the year I was born)
pinned proudly on his porkpie hat,
lunchbox cradled under his arm.
He had been with the 101st too and wished me luck.
Give 'em hell!
as he disappeared into the Seattle five o'clock rush.
Yeah, I said. Yeah. You bet.

The Nam

First Day, Headquarters Co.
101st Airborne
Phan Rang, Viet Nam

The wounded back from the hospital
readying their rucksacks to return to the line.
Line doggies coming out of the bush.
Their lost year done.
Worn rosaries around their necks.
Christ nailed to a tree.
A man prayed out there.
So many trees out there.
So many nails.

First Night in Viet Nam

Twenty-nine years in the Army.
Had to go to Viet Nam
if he wanted to retire with thirty.
Full Stars and Stripes benefits forever.

I felt sorry for him,
and for the rest of us,
as, long after lights out,
we began crossing out days.

First Encounter

You have stopped for a break, stand up
to put your gear on and hear shots,
see the flash of the muzzles.
You have been followed.
The whiteness of the branches
that have been cut along the way
tells you you're on a new trail,
but the sergeant is a stateside G.I.:
barracks inspections, rules and regs.
You are probably surrounded.
There are five others beside you.
You are twenty-three.
You look quickly around you:
the sky, the trees.
You're far from home.
You know now that your life
is no longer yours.

Lieutenant Green

Green was a prima donna.
Arrogant, contemptuous, two weeks out of OCS.
His eyes rabid, out to make a name for himself in the Nam.
His platoon was spitshine boots, starched fatigues
and snappy (Airborne, Sir!) salutes.
You removed your cap if you entered his barracks.
His first mission came and he marched straight
after a Viet Cong into a disgusting explosion
of rusted bolts, nails, bits of "33 Beer" bottles,
GI junk of a Chinese claymore.

The First

Booker said the first time
he saw somebody killed
a gook came charging,
probably high on grass.
Garcia, the machine gunner, opened up,
and the gook just seemed to hang
in the air as the rounds ripped
through him for what seemed minutes.

Oh, how he had been wronged
by being sent to the Nam.
Booker, who kept live rounds in his weapon
during inspection, hoping for a discharge,
who was so dreadfully fainthearted under fire.

Jimmy

Jimmy was always alone since that day
the VC surrounded his recon team
and he was the one the chopper brought back alive.
His eyes. Those so green, so weary
such inexplicably shattered eyes.
His life awarded him posthumously.
He would haunt himself forever.

Smitty

Smitty was a cocky Carolina country boy
gone city with a deck of cards, charming
soft drawl, slick shuffle,
and a smile as deceiving as his deal.
A dirty detail came up and the only name he knew
was Fernando's, who had joined the Army to become
a citizen, something he would decide against in the end.
That day, after Smitty crawled into the thicket
with his recon team to hide the day away,
a VC sprang up behind them,
dealt Smitty a wild deuce and four bullets.
The chopper brought him back to basecamp
with half his head still somehow clinging.
Fernando, who had been inches away, unbelieving.
Flinched with each deep-heaved tangled sob,
far into the frightened night.

Jerry

Jerry, who was drafted with me,
wrote from Saigon:
Bad chow,
The same bars, bar girls,
Homesick,
A bullshit clerk job,
Boredom.
So much money to be made.
Just bought a refrigerator to sell
at a profit in the black market.
The Army is a real drag.
Though it was, he was sure,
nothing at all like the infantry.

Combat Jones

He came to be known as Combat Jones.
Nothing much of him left
in those splattered hazel eyes
since that day, as the story went,
he ran out of ammo,
swung his entrenching tool madly
in hand to hand combat,
the dead Viet Cong piling at his feet.

McWilliams

McWilliams wanted nothing more in the world
than to get back to the World.
He had dreams of himself in silk underwear.
He cheated at dice and tried to draw disability,
a bad back due to a fall faked out in the field.
He was completely worthless in combat.
But even in the jungle he knew the street.
One day he saw one of the combat engineers
walking into the woods with one of the Montagnard girls.
Next thing he was tailing them,
then another six or seven behind him,
and before you knew it the entire platoon,
some of them lining up twice.

Cookie

Cookie made it no secret he wanted Wallace for President.
So desperate to see action he opened fire
on guard duty at Headquarters Company
when he first got to the Nam,
swearing he had seen several VC near the perimeter.
The only one in our platoon who cut off a Viet Cong's ear,
kept it in alcohol in his footlocker back at basecamp.
He jumped on a grenade trying to win the Congressional,
his dream, but it was a dud; got a Silver Star
and a special R & R to Hong Kong instead.
The one who cried in the chopper that monsoon day
after death had come so close we saw the slant of its eyes.
Once, during an infil swore he saw several VC, crouched quickly,
came so very close to getting a punji stake in the balls.
Got a Purple Heart pinned next to his own, a speech
by a major whose sole duty in the Army it seemed was this.

Booker

Booker had been in the boonies up north
long enough to get jungle rot on both feet
on purpose, but was sent from the hospital
back to the boonies instead of to the world.
When word came down we were going up
to the DMZ, he said DMZ, no,
not Demilitarized, baby,
that's Dead Marine Zone.

Atkins

Atkins was a cowboy from Oklahoma.
How he loved carousing, along with Hicks,
who liked to drop things
so that others would bend over.
He got sent to Armor after Basic,
and then down near the Delta
where soon after
his hair started turning white,
and his face sober.

Hicks

Hicks was the one who shortsheeted everybody,
dropped his soap in the shower intentionally.
He was shipped to a line company in the Nam
when he changed his mind about going Airborne.
Somehow got himself assigned as the Commander's
chauffeur.
Dashed around base camp in a shiny jeep, two small flags
on the bumper rustling briskly.
The General's along with regular stars everywhere.
GOTTA GET THEM DINKS stenciled boldly on the windshield.

Jackie J

Jackie stayed just high enough
on grass and Darvon, especially
the last three or four months.
Wanted nothing more than to return
to the world a war hero, marry
his high school sweetheart.
He would always be All-Conference left end.
Once he was left behind by the choppers
before an infil; so scared
he was vomiting, crying shamefully.
Buddies. We went through AIT and the Nam together.
He invited me to visit him back in the world,
Double date.
Mine the town whore.

Gary

All Gary could talk about was the fragile
brown girl back home he had known
just long enough to maker her believe in love.
In Viet Nam no more than sixteen days,
never took a single malaria pill,
and went out on patrol only once.
After he washed off his camouflage
they shipped him back to the world
green as fresh government issue.

Red, White and Blue

Bob, being the only hope
of Christmas that year,
brought his sow to Pleiku.
Miss America the beautiful,
along with Raquel Welch
wearing the colors.
Cheers for the red,
(her panties when she whirled),
white and blue.

Taipei Girl, R &R

Where did your thoughts wander
that hot July night
you looked out over the empty trainyard?

Did you recall Kaosiung, the happy days
there as a farm girl, long before padded clothes
and English lessons in bed?

Daley

Daley had to hump the boonies with the clap;
his dick hanging out,
wrapped in a plastic bag to catch the drip.
A sorrowful Christ carrying a cross
tattooed on his biceps.

Rodger Young

A Mormon, he could assemble and disassemble any weapon
with the same ease as playing Yankee Doodle
and Dixie simultaneously on the guitar.
The war saddened his conscientious eyes forever.

Interrogations

One
way the Army
got a gook
to talk
was to take
two
up in a chopper
and throw
one
of them
out.

Got a gook who wouldn't talk.
Wired his dick
to a G-47
and cranked like crazy.
Would talk then.
In Vietnamese, English
or Greek.

Tied arms and legs
to four tanks.
Stretched him tight,
tighter till he talked.
After all said,
or, if a woman,
after all said and
done,
then revved the engines,
hauled ass as if
heading to

      Chi Town

Frisco   Philly

      Houston

Bates

Bates was sent out as FO that night.
Then came his pleas.

The VC waiting; his screams tempting us.
Until at last first light,

when his company swept the area,
found his skin beside him like a twin.

Riddle

A star even in combat.
He had been captured, staged
a daring escape from the VC.
Re-upped for six months
when his year ended.
Had been back to the world, a parade.
Everybody's next door neighbor.
His handsome, sparkling sapphire eyes.
A mild, winning smile.
The Silver Star of his hometown.
And when the VC zapped him,
we asked ourselves:
If they could kill him—
what of us?

The War Was Over Suddenly

Right after Thanksgiving the war was over; suddenly
the area next to ours was fenced off.
A holding pen.
There was nothing for them but waiting
until the replacements came in.
The 173rd.
Or what was left of it,
After Dak To.

New Year

December 31st came and three Recon teams went in.
Miller's made contact only a short distance form us.
The choppers came in to exfil them.
Midnight.
The sky full of tracers.
The door gunners' M-60s ringing in the new year.
This a time of truce.

Benny

The Viet Cong shot down a chopper one night,
only a few clicks from base camp.
Three recon squads sent in at dawn.
Benny came back unbelieving,
never before so sick to his stomach.
The pilot charred black as a brother.
Benny a brother black as an M-16.

Hooper

Hooper came twice within a step of dying.
Once was in Brooklyn working as a hodcarrier,
fifty stories up.
The people below small as insects
when the scaffolding teeter-tottered under him suddenly.
The second time was in the Nam,
bullets whispering violently by
as he pushed himself as deeply as he could
against the ground.
Here, the smallest of insects
large as automobiles
darting on blades of grass.

Natural History

To cross a river meant leeches.
A company of NVAs crashing towards you
would be a troupe of baboons.
A green snake named Mr. Two Step,
for the number you'd last after bitten.
It was said the NVAs carried flashlights.
One night frightening scores of them
turned out to be a swarm of fireflies.
The whir of birds' wings
turned out to be artillery rounds.
Threw stones at a cobra once,
the sun going down. Fire at it
and the VC would know our position.
A VC moving slowly in the elephant grass
happened to be a water buffalo.
One night they overran the compound.
Loaded down with grenades, AK 47s
from North Viet Nam, mines strapped to their chests:
these were only the mosquitos.
The VC only a little more than a whisper's reach away,

we called in the Cobras. They came in hissing,
cannons twice as fast as the old gunships.
It was also said the VC kept chickens leashed to strings.
So easily frightened they were perfect warning.
One night, shivering uncontrollably with fear,
knowing I would have to kill whatever was out there,
walking slowly, scratching.

Seasons

The dry season was good.
You could hear the VC,
the crackling of leaves, twigs.
They also heard you.

Monsoon came.
The leaves, ground, soft.
The VC couldn't hear you.
Nor you them.

Recondo Sergeant

Only he could draw perfect circles
on the blackboard.
And in the constellations
to steer us out of the jungle.
Told us one way of keeping warm during monsoon
was to piss in our pants.

War Story

Those from the
Big Red 1
said

it was
a
bitch

down
in the
Delta

Wet
day and
night

The water
2 feet
high

in the
dry
places.

Lieutenant Whitman

Out in the boonies in monsoon.
Pissing in our pants to stay warm.
One night the thunk of Viet Cong mortar
no more than fifty yards away.
Next day the lieutenant outraged
because we hadn't moved in instantly,
captured weapons, come away with a body count,
brought him closer to being captain.
He the one who once and only
went on a mission with Smitty's squad.
Within hours was on the radio,
night falling quickly.
The NVA flashlights glowing brighter, closer.
His voice crackling, desperately, as he called
basecamp for a chopper to exfil him.

Stucky

Stucky sawed the handle of his M-79
into a pistol grip.
In the boonies for four months,
then back in camp one day
started bringing, taking the lieutenant's tray
from the mess tent
and got transferred to the supply room.
Kissed the war's ass goodby.

ARVN Rangers

A group of ARVN Rangers came to train with us.
Their sergeant a Tae Kwan Do expert.
They did PT early in the morning, rappelled and etc.
When it came time to go to the boonies
one of them refused.
The sergeant stood him at attention in front of everybody,
hit him with a stick, cursed him fiercely,
then waved the chopper off.
Had him dig a hole just large enough,
gave him rations and water,
covered it with a scrap sheet of tin.
He slept two long cold nights there.
But no way would that ever equal even a minute
of my having to be there fighting his war.

POW

One day suddenly he was in the compound,
a rope tied around his neck, the other end to a stake.
Nothing but several layers of concertina wire,
and a pair of gym trunks to hide him
as we stopped to gawk to and from the mess tent.
Word had it he was a spy, that the Special Forces captain
had promised to take him out first thing in the morning,
and put a .45 to his head.
Next morning not a trace of him
as we passed by on our way to breakfast.
Everybody shaking their heads in admiration.
The captain sure a man of his word all right.

Garbage Detail

They arrived almost faster than the flies.
We shouted at them over and over to get back, cursed
them, and whatever it was put us on garbage detail
in a place called Viet Nam
warning peasants fighting over foodscraps
we would not dump the barrels
if they failed to return the bullets
they found, and might turn over to the VC.

Sergeant Starling

Sergeant Starling taught us to read a trail
not by looking directly in front of you,
but by looking far ahead and tracing back.
He could track the VC as if walking in their shadow.
We would come out of the boonies, be assigned to KP,
and curse the Army even more.
He would always tell us far better
KP than KIA.

Johnny Johnson

The last thing anybody would've called Johnny
was a gung ho GI. He hated the Army.
Had a brother in the Nam
so really didn't have to be in the war.
The last I heard of him
he was sporting a large necklace of rotting ears,
his M-16 steady on Rock 'n Roll.

Lieutenant Karsh

The new lieutenant was so desperate to see action
he transferred from recon to a line company.
In time the sight of so much death
turned him a ghastly shade of yellow
he wore as proudly
as his dress khakis.

Steele

Intelligence had heard for several days
that we would be hit any night
and Steele shows up that day
somehow without an M-16.
That night the perimeter guards
fired a few rounds, nothing else.
Steele pleading hysterically for a razor,
just a straight razor, as if
this was a rumble with the VC back in Philly.

La Russa

La Russa spent the last half of his tour
in Recon, with diarrhea.

How he hated that sergeant,
who had, every day on the line,
made everybody use their drinking water
to shave.

La Russa, of course, looked like a Roman statesman.
One who, immediately after shaving,
appeared never to have shaved at all.

Motto

If it wasn't the VC wanting to blow your shit away
it was the Army insisting this was still the Army.
There were Rules and Regulations.
Used to be a saying in Viet Nam.
What can they do—
send me to Viet Nam?

Turner

Toward the end of his tour
he spent more and more time
in the lieutenant's tent.
One day convinced him,
or perhaps tired him
with self-important smooth talk,
to requisition some plastic explosives
to blow up a cave under a waterfall
he had come across on his last infil.
No more perfect place
for a weapons cache existed, ever.
Problem was the current was so strong
he couldn't take two steps upstream,
so we were forced to scrap the mission.
Booker, who was transferred to recon
after he got jungle rot on both feet
on purpose trying to get back to the world,
regretted he wasn't back on the line,
where Turner would've been dusted
for volunteering troops without their knowledge.

Some would say, I'm sure, Turner was too smart
for his own good; perhaps not smart enough.
Certainly he never had the kind of luck
he desperately needed to become heroic.

Iron Thunder

At eighteen his face already the color of cheap wine,
Sgt. Brashears had disciplined him
in front of the company for drunkenness,
threatened him with a Dishonorable Discharge,
would deny him the opportunity to become a warrior.
Legend has it he was last seen in the Nam
quietly tying what remained of his leg together.

Birdshit, Ham and
Lima Beans and Heroism

What they said in the Army about the Airborne:
>Only two things fall from the sky:
>Fools
>and birdshit

Worst C-Rations ever
were Ham and Lima Beans
Tasted so bad
they were called
Ham and Motherfuckers

Two ways of winning a medal
if you wanted to be a hero:
alive, or as they said in the Nam,
posthumorously

Major Gordon Granger

The major smoked a riverboat gambler's stogie,
wore a .38 gunslinger style, a scalping knife.
Volunteered his line doggies anytime,
kept them in the boonies trying for a higher body count.
Saw him at the airport at Cam Ranh Bay,
dress khakis, rows of medals, going home,
looking for souvenirs, great stories for his grandchildren.
He never left basecamp except for quick scouting trips
on his chopper, always with a gunship or two along.

Peetie

I

Peetie had fewer days left than I had months.
The night before he left
told me about saying goodbye to his good buddy, Robert,
the only other Indian he had known in the Nam.
When the chopper came, Robert took off his steel pot,
something they told you never to do out in the field,
his head full of tomorrows back in the world,
and then a sniper—
Peetie said he threw up and then cried like never before.

II

Somehow Peetie had become good friends with Miller,
the rodeo cowboy, shared picture after picture of his wife
with him, and Miller teased him that he would rope her away,
and when he got back to the world and went to visit Peetie,
did so.

Eddie

After all the shit out in the boonies he got KP
and after a while flung away trays,
and scrub brush, and without a word
grabbed his M-16, a bandoleer,
fired up the First Sergeant,
walked out to the perimeter,
fired until his company added one more gook
to its body count,
only this one's name was Eddie.

The Last Detail

In the boonies with Charlie
trying to blow your shit away
for a year.
You came out
and the Army had one last detail:
Had you burning the shit of the Vietnamese workers
in cut-off fifty-five gallon drums.

Last Day in Viet Nam

It was either a sweep and mop up operation
through the barracks of our last sleep in the Nam
or have our orders canceled.
One quick stroke of the pen
was all that was necessary.
Forget that freedom bird waiting.
For the pen, vowed the sergeant,
is mightier than the sword.

The Years After

Home Finally Going Home

We landed at Ft. Lewis,
got measured, issued new dress uniforms
and sent to the Mess Hall, choice USA steaks.
A sergeant said Pass me the salt, boy
to a corporal, and he did.
Outside the buses waiting
to take us to the airport.
We were home finally going home.

Forbidden Openings

He said he had some pretty good pictures
of confirmed kills.
Asked if I cared to see them
in a tone used for propositioning.
Framed next to his Bronze Star, his Campaign Medal,
a writhing entanglement of flesh.
Eyes frozen in burning passion.
The forbidden openings of bodies
made many by M-16s.

Kirby

Kirby knew tobacco; according to him
you seeded your crops next to a hillside
planted with plenty of junked cars.
That way, when it rains the water rushes down
and the rust makes the leaves
right heavy come market time.

We were lucky he didn't get us killed,
(and he that we didn't kill him),
he snored so loudly his turns on guard duty.

Right now he's back in Kentucky
recounting his lost year in the Nam; silver wings
his name, "Rebel Paratrooper," along with the obvious
Confederate flag unfurled across his bony forearm;
still sucking on Winstons.

Garland Finerty

He supervises a parking lot in DC
Will call out to you as you pass by,
give you some money for a meal.
You're in the Airborne and far from home.
He has an album, hundreds of photos
of paratroopers, Green Berets he's befriended.
Hopes you'll come on over to his place in Virginia,
Fly with him far into ecstasy on silver wings.

Leone

Leone wasn't supposed to be in the Army.
Lied to the Draft Board
because he wanted to go to Viet Nam and fight,
prove he was worthy of being a citizen.
Didn't want to be just another Italian.
A year after he came home I read in the Tribune
he was told he could remain seated for the ceremony,
but had insisted on standing on his artificial legs
so that some judge in Jersey
could declare him an American.

Seen on a T-Shirt Superimposed on a Map of Viet Nam, Albuquerque, Summer, 1980:

Participant

Southeast Asia
War Games

1968-1969

Second Place

Hancock

The last time he set foot in the Delta.
Shrapnel so small a year later
you first said to yourself,
an explosion of blackheads across his face.
Gone too the girlish curls, charming Billy smile.
He talked about taking his disability check,
moving as far away from America as Australia.
To this day, his legs still Missing in Action.

Gooks

To Miller war was one more rodeo.
A good ole boy from back home,
who talked the brass into awarding him a Silver Star
for firing up a squad of NVAs
we had evaded earlier that morning.
Cookie, the radioman, swore they had the LZ surrounded.
Miller recommended me for a Bronze Star
for throwing a White Phosphorous grenade
before jumping into the chopper.
On R & R in Taipei he turned to me
during The Return of the Magnificent Seven,
said Yul Brynner's only hope
was to put the gooks to work fortifying the village.
Late one night I burned the orders for the Bronze Star.
When orders for a Bronze Star burn,
you suddenly notice the smoke curls beautifully,
spirals like the smoke from the star-spangled bursts
of white phosphorous, especially
when you're trying to get painfully drunk
on cheap red wine, just home from Viet Nam.

The Bread of Noon

A restaurant in Munich.
An afternoon in late July.
The sadness of a day in fall.
The sadness of these men who became men
in a war the year I was born.
These the men who bore weapons of steel
blue as their eyes for the fatherland.
Eyes that stalked men, perhaps my uncles,
through the sights of their rifles.
They laugh manly laughs, tease the homely waitress,
raise tall glasses of beer golden as their hair.
Somewhere in this country there stood a bridge
that long ago was destroyed by dynamite.
Grandfather's nephew broken
easily as the bread of this noon.

The Years After

Twenty years after Viet Nam
I still walk the jungle in camouflage.
My M-16 mind on recon patrol
on city streets, in restaurants, bars,
during breakfast, at work.
Neighbors, relatives, friends,
everybody has slant eyes.
I watch their movement.
Record everything in notebooks.

Twenty-one years after Viet Nam
where friendly woodchoppers by day
would be VC at night
I'm still on recon patrol.
Everybody has slant eyes.
It's an M-16 world.
Teacher by day,
tonight I'm at the trigger
of an electric typewriter.
This paper has yellow skin.
These poems have slanted eyes.

Epilogue

An Open Letter to President Bush:

Perhaps if you
knew how much,
how much
I wept,
these past months,
so full of rage, another war,

Perhaps if you
knew that our son
almost died in infancy, twice;
his mother and I do not want
him harmed; you cannot
have him, another war,

Perhaps if you
knew how much
I prayed all through Catholic school,
but never like that day,
the VC so close, we trembled
uncontrollably in the mud, another war,

Perhaps if you
had seen Cookie,
who carried a metal-covered-Bible
next to his heart, break down
and cry unashamedly in the chopper,
at the end of that day, another war,

Perhaps if you
met my daughters;
one has long elegant fingers,
a lunar near her upper lip; the other,
large dark eyes, sprawling eyelashes;
50,000 body bags ordered, another war,

Perhaps if you,
then perhaps
you might not
make war
seem so unbelievably
easy.

Leroy V. Quintana

Leroy V. Quintana was born in Albuquerque, New Mexico in 1944, and was raised in Raton, New Mexico. He left the University of New Mexico for the Army, Airborne, and went to Viet Nam with the 101st, transferring to a Long-Range Reconnaissance Patrol (LRRP) unit. He spent a year in Viet Nam (1967-68) and finished his Army career at Ft. Bragg, NC. After leaving the military he completed his B.A. in English in 1971. In 1970 he was married to Yolanda Holguin, and they have two daughters—Sandra and Elisa—and a son, Jose. He received an M.A. in English in 1973 from New Mexico State University, and a later earned a second M.A. in Psychology/Counseling from Western New Mexico University. He has worked as a full time mental health counselor and as an educator. He is a tenured Associate Professor at San Diego Mesa College. His poems have appeared in anthologies and journals, and he is the author of *Hijo del Pueblo, Sangre*, and the forthcoming *Now and Then, Often, Today.*